A Dartford Survival Guide

Ayla Uzunhasan, Diana Mote, Michael Golson and Ciaran McWilliams

College Books

British Library Cataloguing Publication Data.
A catalogue record for this book is available from the British Library

Published by College Books – www.nwkmedia.com

ISBN : 978-1-907502-11-8

North West Kent College
Dartford
Kent

Contents

Welcome!

Hello! Welcome to your very own guide to the *ahem* spectacular town which goes by the name of Dartford. Situated in Kent, Dartford is a popular town with the youth because of the nightlife and the fact that Bluewater (the second largest shopping centre in the UK) is literally 10 minutes up the road! Other than that, admittedly Dartford has not much else to offer on the interesting front. You have a fairly nice typical park, the football team (yes, Dartford F.C. does exist!) and the usual things a usual town has. We are actual students of North West Kent College, located In Dartford, so we are able to share first hand views on what it's actually like to study in the area. Dartford is a place where young and old reside, a town where everyone is welcome and generally a good place to kind of be. We are here to provide you an up-to-date survival guide, whether you're looking to visit, study or happen to accidently end up here. We have everything covered in how to make the most of your time in Dartford and of course how to survive it...

Basics

History

Dartford goes way back to the Roman and Saxon era and has seen to have achieved roads and villas whilst also going through two World Wars in the 20th century. Humans have only lived in the local area for 250, 000 years which only seems a short amount time compared to the world existing for millions of years. Here is a timeline of what Dartford has been through over the many years:

Prehistoric

The *Old Stone Age* (Palaeolithic), the *Middle Stone Age* (Mesolithic), and the *New Stone Age* (Neolithic). *Bronze Age* and *Iron Age* - Before man discovered how to use bronze and iron he made all of his tools from wood, stone and bone. Many remains from the Palaeolithic, Mesolithic, and Neolithic eras have been found around Dartford.

Romans

As the first place invaded, Kent is one of the richest in Roman remains. Important sites have been found along the length of the River Darent; at Dartford, Wilmington, Farningham and Lullingstone. Other evidence of Roman life has been found in Ash, Longfield, Joydens Wood and Springhead.

Saxons

Once the Romans left, the villas and roads fell into ruin and the populous forgot Roman skills and technology. The Saxons lived in sunken huts made from timber they was called Grubenhaus. The Saxon buildings did not last over time and the only evidence left is the post holes left in the ground. Most evidence is from what the Saxons left in their cemeteries and some of the largest are found around the Dartford area.

Normans

The Norman attack occurred in 1066, and was led by Duke William who later became known has William the Conqueror. The Normans built many churches, castles and cathedrals. Holy Trinity church was built in c.1080 under the supervision of Bishop Gundulf who also watched over the construction of Rochester Cathedral, and the Tower of London. It was probable that the church was a defense overlooking the ford over the River Darent.

Medieval

Medieval times in Dartford, between East Hill and West Hill, were cut in two by the Rivers Darent and Cranpit. Later it became the town sewer, and the Darent, which was much wider and gave access to the Thames by boat. A footbridge was built across the Darent in c.1400. Before this time people had to seek out a hermit to ferry them across the river. The yearly cost of getting across the river was 13 shillings and 4 pence (about 62 pence today).

Tudor

The Tudor period was from 1485 to 1603, during that time the layout of Dartford can only be guessed at, as only one part of a map from 1596 survived. Some of the Tudor buildings are still standing today and a few of the modern façades hide Tudor beams and plaster. Tudor Dartford covered the High Street, Spital Street, Hythe Street, Bullace Lane, Lowfield and Overy Street. The High Street had many large timber-framed buildings (many of which survived to the 19th century) and was a busy thoroughfare. Increased urbanisation and the poor sanitation led to many diseases. As well as the Plague new diseases entered England in the Tudor period; smallpox and sweating sickness which could kill a victim in two to three hours. Untreated sewage, offal, dung and germs carried by the rivers of Dartford, led to typhus, cholera and dysentery.

World War One

Local people knew Britain was at war with Germany when London buses carrying troops passed through the town on their way to Dover. At the start of the war a barricade was placed across the Brent near the entrance to Hesketh Park. Armed soldiers patrolled this barricade and stopped every vehicle that passed through. September 1914 saw the formation of the Dartford Division Recruiting Committee and many local men signed up. Many of those volunteers were killed in France and Belgium in the trenches.

World War Two

Dartford was the most heavily bombed area per acre in Britain. The town suffered much destruction and loss of life when it served as the front line for the German bombardment of Britain. Planes which could not make it to London often dumped their bombs on Dartford before returning home.

Since the wars, Dartford has developed more in technology and mechanically. Intelligence has improved (for some) and everyone is able to live in better conditions. Please read on and get a taster for Dartford and see if it's the place for you.

So, to start we'll look at some facts about Dartford. This can be boring so we've tried to make it as interesting as possible; usually facts only interest certain people, so if you are that certain person who loves facts please read on!

Factfile

Roughly 85,900 people live here
It has a historic museum, a library, the Miskin Theatre and the Mick Jagger Centre.
Featured on popular films, programmes and adverts including Harry Potter, The Inbetweeners and on the advertisement for the Crunchy Nut Cereal.
It's also the home town to Mick Jagger and Keith Richards from The Rolling Stones

A thing you need to know:

- The people may seem weird, however they often are very nice.

Kent County Council

The council is responsible for public services such as education, transport, strategic planning, emergency services, social services, public safety and waste disposal.

The role of this department is to encourage people of all ages and backgrounds to play active roles in their communities; for example we have adult education, cultural & sports development and youth support. Kent Youth County Council is for the younger people ages 11-18 to be able to speak out to their county for issues they may have.

Dartford Borough council take cares of the town's affairs as well as the local villages that surround the area such as Stone, Bean, Darenth, Longfield & New Barn, Southfleet, Sutton-at-Hone & Hawley, Swanscombe, Greenhithe and Wilmington.

The population of the Borough is roughly 85,900 residents and approximately 37,400 households. Dartford is located on the border of Kent, London and Essex. The town is one of the most exciting and dynamic area's in the country. The local council are looking to see if there are living zones able to grow around 20,000 new homes and up to 50,000 new jobs created in the borough over the next 25 years in addition to the existing 80,000 residents in the Borough. However, as well as developing the region the council is working on making the town a safer and more pleasant place for the current and future residents by improving on anti-social behavior. By having the *"Not Wanted"* campaign the message that the council is trying to get across is that disrupting the residents is not okay. This is mainly aimed at graffiti and drinking on the streets.

Mrs. Ann Allen is a retired catering officer for the Dartford Hospital. She lists her interests as her grandchildren and gardening, and is actively involved in many local voluntary groups and organisations. Among these are:

- Trustee of the Dartford Almshouse Charity
- Wilmington Parochial Charity
- Homestart
- KCHT
- Dartford Almshouse Charity
- Wilmington Parochial Charity
- Member of Groundwork Kent, Medway & Dartford CAB
- Chairperson of the Dartford Age Concern
- KCC Member
- Equality and Diversity Champion

She was also elected to the County Council in May 1997, as the Conservative Member for Dartford South West.
She gained a City and Guilds Certificate in hotel and catering management which enabled her to work in all aspects of catering. She is also a former foster worker.

Mrs. Allen has served as a Parish and District Councilor. She is the Member of Dartford Borough Council for Joydens Wood and the Cabinet Member for the Communities and Wellbeing Portfolio. She served the Council since 1985, and was named 'Woman of the Year' in 1994 for her services to the community.

She was the Deputy Mayor in 1992/93 and the Mayor of Dartford in 1993/94.

Interview with Mrs. Allen

Have you lived in Dartford all your life?
Yes.

Have you always wanted to work for the council?
No, I was involved in my local community; the local play group and voluntary work. I had my own catering business part time whilst looking after my family.

How did you come about working for the council?
I was asked by the Conservative Party. 50 years ago, I was interested with the Lib Dems, but was influenced by lots of strikes in the docks and saw the impact and damaged effect on the country and made me recognize that the Conservatives were fitting with my outlook.

What was it like to be Mayor of Dartford?
It was a great honor being the Queens representative and meeting and greeting people in Dartford.

How has Dartford changed over the last 50 years?
We have had the Dartford tunnel, Dartford bridge, M25, Bluewater, Darenth Valley hospital and a new football stadium.

What does Dartford need more of to make it more appealing to tourists?
I don't think Dartford needs anything. It has got nice gardens and parks to walk in, the Thames and a good area to shop and Bluewater is up the road.

Places

Library

All libraries within Dartford, including mobile libraries, records offices and archives are managed by Kent County Council. It has many sections on different subjects from history, languages, travel and children's books. The library also provides computers. The local museum in Market Street is housed in the same building as the library

Sunday – Closed
Monday – Friday 8.30am – 6.00pm
Saturday 9.00pm

Shopping

Shopping, you either love it or hate it but at the end of the day you kind of have to do it!

So why not take the time to have a look round the main centres: the Orchards shopping centre and the Priory. The main shops include the *very posh* Waitrose, Boots, New Look and a few too many coffee shops including Love Coffee. You will find all your typical high street stores and more. Or perhaps you're into your vintage/cheap/one-of-a-kind bargains? I know for a fact that with the number of Charity shops around you will be guaranteed to find something. Although these are the clothes from the people who live here so if you're not too bothered about fashion then you will love these shops (hint: apparently it's best to look round early on Saturday mornings!). Obviously if you're a shopaholic, Dartford doesn't really provide any *good* shops, so thankfully Bluewater is very close!

Bluewater is a huge shopping centre packed with everything from the Cinema, to restaurants and also a great range of shops. If you're lucky you could possibly spot a famous face once in a while too, they love to hang out there. Of course, if none of these take your fancy you could get a train and go into London Town, but that defeats the whole purpose of this book; however it's still an option.

Weekends

Everyone lives for the weekend, right? So what better place to spend yours! With countless of clubs, pubs and bars you're sure to have a *very interesting* night! These places are the best to go if you're into dancing, music and generally just having a good time. The club life in Dartford is cheap and fun! The music is bang on trend, the scene is lively and generally most people can enjoy a good night clubbing here in Dartford. One of the favourites is Air & Breath; however there are a few more you might enjoy, such as:

Clubs:

- **Air & Breathe**
- **Bar Mondo's**
- **Crush**

These three are the most popular clubs you will find in Dartford, each one unique however still carrying that Dartford vibe!

Air and Breath (Zens): A night club, more popular with the younger adults. It has a small layout but as you walk in you have a long bar to your right and straight ahead is the dance floor where you're going to be! For you Hip–Hop lovers and R'n'b grinders there is a room upstairs where you can bust some moves and a smaller bar where you can listen to the music you like.

Bar Mondo's: Bar Mondo's is a small bar situated in Dartford town. It's popular with the music scene as there are DJ's, Club nights and live acoustic music. It is a great place for a band to perform and get their name out there; however even though the bar is small it still creates a great atmosphere. I definitely recommend it for people who like music and being social.

Crush: The club is a lovely venue and just the right size with a funky disco-like dance floor! The place has a big garden with an outside bar and loads of comfy seating for you smokers. I would recommend Fridays for 18 -25 and Saturdays for 26 - 35 because you don't want to look like a loner!

And obviously if none of these take you're fancy find a friend and then find a Dartford house party! These are likely to entertain everyone, however make sure you know the people as we wouldn't want to start any trouble now would we?!

However if your looking for a good pub to chill out in, these are some of the local friendly ones were you can enjoy a good pint, with good company and sometimes good music.

Pubs:

- **The Courthouse**
- **The Cressy Arms**
- **The Flying Boat**
- **Harvester**
- **The Odd Fellows**

Parks

It's always nice in the summer to gather a few friends, a partner or family and sit in a park watching the clouds and eating ice-cream! The parks in Dartford are big, green and lovely to do exactly that in them. There are two major parks: Central Park (in Market Street) and Hesketh Park (in Park Road) and a few other green areas such as Darenth Woods, Dartford Heath and Beacon Wood Country Park. Central Park includes a child's play area, a skateboard park and a fully enclosed ball game area. Hesketh however differs in a way as it is dominated by more sporting activities such as cricket and tennis, it also includes a children's playground and a sun dial is located at the Northern

end of the park. The parks can hold some unwanted rubbish, smells and even people but if you're able to avoid them at all costs you could manage to have a great time.

Best places to eat

So you're on your break from college or even shopping, or you even fancy spending a night out having dinner – but where to choose? We've picked some of the best places in Dartford to have a good old feast so you don't have to. Of course Dartford provides the usual food chains including:

- **Wimpy**
- **McDonalds**
- **KFC**
- **Greggs'**
- **Dominos**
- **Subway**
- **Harvester**

Bluewater and places around the Dartford area also offer many independent places to eat out in, however these are just a few of our recommendations.

Fish and Chips
Brent fish bar, Mr Chippy

Chinese
Four seasons, Golden City

Indian
Ghandi's Spice, Goan Spice

There are also many coffee and Cafes around town, most popular on a Sunday morning of course:

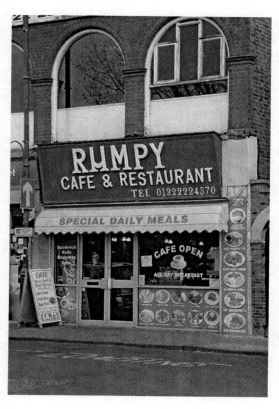

- **Ossies Café**
- **Costa Coffee**
- **All Day Café**
- **The Coffee House**
- **Kells Café**

Dartford has some great cafes, full of the best hangover curing food and cheap drinks. Visit All Day Café for an amazing breakfast for a really food value, with friendly staff and a warm feel or try out The Coffee House for a good cup of Coffee and maybe a cheeky muffin. Make sure you do it!

Transport in Dartford

Travelling by Car:

Dartford has quite a few low cost car parks dotted around the town centre, the main ones being the Orchards shopping centre, a multi-story car park by Kent Road as well as one by the Priory centre.

Dartford is linked to London via the A2 which links Dartford to the Kent Coast via the M2 motorway which leads to Canterbury, as well as Dover.

The Dartford Tunnel and the Queen Elizabeth II bridge gains access to Essex.

The southern section of the M25 gains access to the M20 to Maidstone, Folkestone and Dover as well as the M23 to Gatwick Airport and Brighton.

Travelling by Bus:

Most buses in the Dartford area are run by the Arriva Bus Company although others could be run by Transport of London, which run through Dartford to and from London.

Dartford routes: 126, 160, 162, 233, 286, 428, 492, B12 and the B13.

Travelling by Train:

Dartford station is the nodal point for three lines from London:

- North Kent Line (via Woolwich Arsenal)
- Bexleyheath Line.
- Dartford Loop Line (via Sidcup)

Dartford station is a major interchange station in the North Kent region of the Southeastern network.

The station is famous for being the place where *Mick Jagger* and *Keith*
Richards met each other for the first time since their school days. This chance meeting would result in the forming of the rock band *The Rolling Stones.*

Things To Do

Events

If you're planning to make your time at Dartford more permanent or you happen to be in the area around these times then be sure to check the events out! (Well face it, there's not much else to do!)

Dartford Festival

Dartford festival is held each year in the summer! Dancing, sporting events, library in the park (don't ask!), fairground rides and celebrities are some of the things included in this unique event! Be sure not to miss the famous singers and entertainers who perform, past performers have been Xfactor and Britain's Got Talent contestants so if you like that sort of thing make sure you attend this festival. If you're wandering how to get there here are some details taken from the website:

- By Bus:423, 433, 489, 414, 455, 477, 480, 490 & Fastrack
- By Rail: Dartford BR Station.
- Disabled parking via. Cranford Road, Dartford, DA1 1JP
- Festival Car Parking In Acacia Hall, High Street, Dartford, DA1 1DJ.
- Parking costs: £3.00 per car.

The Orchard Theatre

The Orchard Theatre, located in the town centre, is a fully professional theatre, providing audiences with a large range of drama, dance, music and entertainment. The theatre opened in September 1982 and quickly gained a reputation as one of the country's premier venues presenting a remarkable range of entertainment.

The theatre has had some great shows/pantos from Beauty and the Beast to Jimmy Carr. Every year there is always a Christmas panto to fit for the family.

The Miskin Theatre

The Miskin theatre is located in North West Kent College. Students put on shows, where anyone is welcome to come and see how hard the students have been working. They put on well known show such as Peter Pan and The Wind in the Willows. (Tickets are available online at miskintheatre.com)

People & Culture

Believe it or not, Dartford does have some claim to fame. Here are some famous people who have or had some sort of connection with Dartford:

Mick Jagger & Keith Richards

Probably the most well known celebrities from Dartford are the founders of the rock band *The Rolling Stones*, front man Mick Jagger and guitarist Keith Richards.

Both were born in the Dartford area and the two met when they attended Wentworth Primary school. Jagger was born into a middle class family, where his musical talents were encouraged and he eventually left Primary school having passed his eleven-plus to get into Dartford Grammar school.

Richards started playing guitar at the age of 16 which he acquired by swapping a pile of records for with a friend. His mother would often try and influence his musical taste by introducing him to such artists as Billie Holiday, Louis Armstrong and Duke Ellington. His father was less encouraging, telling him to *"Stop that bloody noise!"* After Primary school he attended Dartford Technical School, and so Jagger and Richards lost contact as they were at different schools.

Years later, the two met by chance on the platform at Dartford Station. Richards noticed the *Chuck Berry* and *Muddy Waters*

LP's Jagger was carrying with him, and two realised they had a mutual interest in Rhythm and Blues music. This was the start of a re-established friendship that started *The Rolling Stones.*

The Rolling Stones have established themselves as one of the biggest rock bands of all time, having released 22 studio albums. Jagger and Richards are considered one of the greatest song writing partners ever and are often compared to Lennon and McCartney of *The Beatles.* Along with *The Beatles*, they were part of the "British - Invasion" of popular British bands in America in the 1960s.

They are the second most successful group in the Billboard Hot 100 chart and were ranked the 4th greatest artist in Rolling Stone magazines 100 Greatest Artists of All-Time.

Other Dartford Celebrities

Dartford has been associated with quite a few famous faces and a few sports stars in recent years. Here are a few of the ones you may know…

Anne of Cleves

King Henry VIII's forth wife Anne of Cleves is probably most famous for being described as a "Flanders mare" by the King, who had only ever seen beautiful paintings of her before they met. Their marriage only lasted 6 months before it was annulled, but the she was allowed to stay in England by the King, where she remained all her life. She lived in many different houses owned by the King, one of them being the Dartford Manor House, where she stayed between 1553 and 1557. Part of the house still stands today and can be seen by its East side from Hythe Street.

Peter Blake

Sir Peter Blake is an artist who's primary style is pop art. He is best know for his iconic sleeve design for The Beatles "Sgt. Pepper's Lonely Hearts Club Band" LP. Peter Blake has worked on record sleeves for other musicians such as Paul Weller's "Stanley Road", The Who's "Face Dances" and the sleeve for Band Aid's charity single "Do They Know It's Christmas?". Peter Blake was given a CBE in 1983 and received a knighthood in 2002 for his services to art. More recent work of his includes a collage for Chelsea F.C for the 2010 season.

Margaret Thatcher

Margaret Thatcher is a former Prime Minister and former leader of the Conservative Party. "The Iron Lady", as she was nicknamed, was the first woman in the UK to lead a major political party, and the UK's first ever female Prime Minister. Her reign as Prime Minister lasted from 1979 – 1990. In the general elections in 1950 and 1951, she campaigned for a seat in Dartford with the Labour party. This attracted media attention due to her being the youngest and the only female campaigning for a seat, despite this she lost both times to Norman Dodds. During these campaigns, she met Denis Thatcher, who she would marry in 1951 and have twins, Carol and Mark, in 1953.

Andy Fordham

2004 World Darts Champion Andy Fordham is probably more famous for his time spent on *Celebrity Fit Club* than for his Darts. But in Dartford he is a bit of legend. Known as "The Viking", Andy and his wife Jenny moved to Dartford in 2001 to run the "*The Rose*" pub to try and encourage a normal life with a normal job to go along with his Darts fame.

Glen Johnson

Glen Johnson, the current Liverpool and England right-back has a claim to fame in the Dartford area. In January 2007, Johnson was caught stealing a toilet seat from the Dartford B&Q, despite reportedly earning £30, 000 a week in wages. The England star and fellow football star Ben May were caught by a 74 year old security guard trying to put a toilet seat in a box with a cheaper price tag, along with hiding taps underneath a sink to avoid paying for it. "We all recognised Johnson," said one worker at the store. "No one could quite believe a bloke like him, with all that money would be moronic enough to nick a toilet seat." They seemed to find the whole thing funny and couldn't stop smirking even after they had been arrested."

Dartford F.C.

Dartford F.C. is Dartford's very own football club. The club plays their home games at the eco-friendly Prince's Park stadium. If you're interested in football, you should check them out.

History

Dartford F.C. Was originally formed by members of Dartford Workingmen's club in 1888. The club started off playing friendly games, but soon entered into cup games, in which they reached the final of the Kent Senior Cup in 1894. The club would enter the Kent League as a Founder-Member in 1894, until October 1895 when Dartford F.C. played their first game in the FA Cup.

Two seasons later, the club would go on to become Founder-Members of the Southern League Division Two, in which they won the championship on their first attempt. For the seasons following after, Dartford F.C. would move between the Southern and Kent leagues before dropping into the West Kent League after financial problems. At this time, the club had also found its very first permanent home ground; Summers Meadow. The club rejoined Kent league after winning the West Kent league and the Cup 'double' during 1908-09. Dartford F.C. remained here until the start of the First World War.

Dartford won the Kent league cup in 1923-24 before moving to the Southern league for the 1926-27 season. The Dartford Board appointed Bill Collier as the manager of Dartford F.C., who had previous success with Kettering Town F.C. Collier's success had also carried over to Dartford, as the club won the Southern league Eastern section title in 1930-31 and 1931-32. Dartford almost won a third time in a row, but missed by one point. The club had also won the overall championship, and winning the Kent Senior League four times during five seasons and the Senior Shield three times.

The clubs reputation would grow nationally, as they had become the first club outside of the Football league that reached the third round of the FA Cup. Bill Collier resigned from the club at the end of the decade, taking his success with him, as Dartford F.C. saw out the decade a lot quieter than they had started. Dartford would show little success from 1939 – 1945.

After Bill Collier, Warney Cresswell was assigned as the manager of the club. Dartford had very little success to show, and Warney Cresswell was replaced with Bill Moss. This decision managed to put some stability back into the club. Dartford F.C. spent the majority of the 1950's and 60's in the Premier Division.

From the start of the 1970's, the club appeared in four Senior Cup finals, wining two of them. They had further success in the 1973-74 season, in which they won the Southern League Championship under the management of Doug Holden but failed to enter the Football League. Ernie Morgan replaced Doug Holden as manager just before the next season. Dartford F.C. failed to enter the Alliance Premier League, they did win their first the Southern League Cup. The team won the Southern Division of the Southern League, eventually managing to get a place in the Alliance Premier League in 1980-81, but this was short lived.

In 1983 Dartford F.C. appointed former Leytonstone manager John Still as manager of the club, which was an instant success and saw the club once again win the Southern League Championship and return to the Alliance Premier League. The club enjoyed a couple of seasons of relative success before they were once again relegated, which saw the end of Still's brief Dartford career. He was replaced by former Tottenham and England winger Peter Taylor in 1986, who served as a player/manager. Taylor managed the club for four seasons, which saw a vast improvement in performances and stadium attendances (which rose from around 450 to 1,000).

In his four seasons in charge, Dartford F.C. finished in the top four of the Southern League Premier Division and scored over one hundred goals a season, a record that still exists today. As well as League success, Taylor's time at Dartford F.C. saw him win the Southern Cup twice, the Kent Senior Cup twice as well as reach the FA Trophy semi-finals twice.

Following the Bradford City stadium fire and the Hillsborough disaster, new rules were introduced where many clubs had to upgrade or relocate their stadiums. Dartford F.C. decided to upgrade their stadium. As a result, the club spent large sums of money on planning and design fees which proved to be a heavy burden on the clubs already hefty deficit. Because of this, rivals Maidstone United, had to share with the club at the start of the 1988/1989 season, but this partnership didn't last long as they announced bankruptcy in 1992 and had to resign from the league.

Dartford F.C. only played the first four games of the 1992/1993 season before withdrawing from the league, after the club was forced to sell their Watling Street stadium to creditors. This started

a twelve year period without a proper home stadium, where the club were forced to stadium share with a variety of local rivals. The start of the 1993/1994 season saw the Darts manage to agree a stadium share agreement with Crays Wanderers and compete in the Kent League with former player Tony Burnham becoming manager. With a couple of seasons of mostly mid-table finishes, the club finally began to challenge for the title and in the 1995/1996 season narrowly missed out on promotion to the Southern League Premier Division on goal difference. However, the following season proved to be more successful as the club finally gained promotion, but saw manager Tony Burnham resign due to business commitments, so reserve team manager Gary Julians took over the helm.

The club managed to consistently finish in the middle of the table over the following seasons, with the best performance coming in the 1999/2000 season where they finished eighth. The start of the 2000/2001 season saw the Darts move closer to home as they stadium shared with bitter rivals Gravesend & Northfleet at the Stonebridge Road stadium. Tony Burnham briefly returned to manage the club before he was replaced by Tommy Sampson and over the next few season's attendances and on field performances improved greatly to stable the clubs financial position.

Midway through the 2003/2004 season it was announced that the Dartford Borough Council had agreed to provide funding and a site for a new home stadium for Dartford F.C. in time for the 2006/2007 stadium. The first game that was played at the new Prince's Park stadium was against Horsham YMCA F.C. and was won 4-2 by the home side in front of a crowd of over 4,000. The stadium received significant publicity in the national press for its environmentally-friendly features. Fashion designer and architect Wayne Hemingway was particularly full of praise for the stadium on the popular morning show *Soccer AM,* whom described the stadium as *"absolutely the number one stadium in the country…"*

By this time Tony Burnham was reinstated as club manager and

Darts performances began to improve. Finally 2009/2010 season saw the club win promotion to the Conference South following their Isthmian League Premier Division victory.

Honours

- FA Trophy Finalists: 1973-74
- Isthmian League Premier Division Champions: 2009-10
- Isthmian League Division One North Champions: 2007-08
- Southern League Champions: 1930-31, 1931–32, 1973–74, 1983–84
- Southern League (Eastern) Champions: 1930-31, 1931–32
- Southern League Southern Division Champions: 1980-81
- Southern League Division Two Champions: 1896-97
- Southern League Cup Winners: 1976-77, 1987–88, 1988–89
- Southern League Championship Match Winners: 1983-84, 1987–88, 1988–89
- Kent Senior Cup Winners: 1930-31, 1931–32, 1932–33, 1934–35, 1946–47, 1967–70, 1972–73, 1986–87, 1987–88
- Kent Senior Trophy Winners: 1995-96
- Kent League Cup Winners: 1924-25
- Kent League Division One Runners Up: 1995-96
- Inter-League Challenge Match Winners: 1973-74 (beat Boston United (NPL) 5-3 on aggregate)

Club Information

Admission Prices

Tickets to see Dartford F.C. are £12 for an adult, £6 for concessions (12 -17 & over 60's) and £2 for a childs ticket (up to 11 years old).

Season tickets and seat reservations are also available on the clubs website.

Dartford F.C. Coach Travel

The club runs a coach service to transport fans to away games. It's £12 for a return ticket and £6 for under 16s. Seats on the coach can be booked by getting in contact with Paul, either directly at home games, phone/text on *07913 391138* (evenings only) or by email dfcawaytravel@aol.com.

Contact Information

Princes Park
Grassbanks
Darenth Road
Dartford
Kent
DA1 1RT

Telephone: 01322 299990
Email: info@dartfordfc.co.uk

General Manager: generalmanager@dartfordfc.co.uk
DFC Reception: claredfcreception@yahoo.co.uk / 01322 299991

Education

The schools and colleges in Dartford are not too bad! Here are a list of schools and colleges situated in the Dartford area:

Dartford Grammar School

Dartford Gramar School for girls

Wilmington Enterprise College

Dartford Techology College

Leigh Technology Academy

North West Kent College

What do students think of studying at Dartford?

If you're reading this as a person looking to move to Dartford, or looking to just be educated here then read on. We have all you need to know on how to survive both college and school. We interviewed a college student to see their view on life as a student here.

Joseph Johnson, 18, Dartford

So Joe you are currently a student at North West Kent College studying Media and it's your second year. Your from the Dartford area did you go to secondary school here?

Yes, I went to Wilmington Hall School. It was quite an experience - I mean we were on the BBC news!

Oh really? Why was that!?

For something quite amazing! For the most students excluded in one day because of the strict uniform rules! One of my friends appeared on the news as I was sitting eating my tea, was quite weird.

Really? Wow, did you ever get excluded?

No, I survived secondary school.

So now you're at college how do you find life as an older student?

I find it more safe, I found a girlfriend at college who I love with my heart and I find life in Dartford a lot calmer and nicer. The people are a bit rough around the edges hence why I don't have many friends. I like the tutors and would say they were my BFFL's (*Best friends for life*) . The fact I can buy cigarettes being 18 now is a TOUCH and having smoking areas in college is great!

What do you do at the weekends, when not at college?

I go to the pub, The Flying Boat, with my other half where we sit and drink wine and sometimes eat crisps. Sometimes on a Saturday night, if im not working at the local pizza shop I go to Air N Breathe, what a club!

And what are the people like at college?

You have to be careful as you do some across a few hooligans!

There has been trouble but you get that anywhere. Sometimes you have to find safe routes as you never know what's round the corner!

And how do you find the education?

What's "education"?

That's Dartford summed up in 2 words.

Fashion

Not sure how to dress when walking the street of Dartford? We're no experts on fashion but we can slightly advice you all about the *fashionistas* that live here!

Girls

This is your stereotypical fashion for a girl. The tracksuit is a popular choice here, in a variation of colours you can really have your pick in which you want. Other options are leggings (with a short, short top).

Make-up is kept to a minimum and hair is usually slicked back or with ratty extensions (dyed).

Boys

This is your stereotypical fashion for a boy. The tracksuit is also a popular choice, as well as caps and trainers. Caps are usually worn right way round, and trainers are <u>never</u> kept white!

Hair is usually gelled underneath the cap and gold chains are a favourite. Staff dogs are usually a good accessory, but not essential.

Of course this is just an opinion and bases solely on the most popular trends, of course some of the youth who live in Dartford do have good fashion and do not fit the category, however they are very rare to find!

The End

So that's it, you've read and learnt all there is to know about Dartford Town. We hope you take everything we've told into consideration and enjoyed our guide! We would be really happy if you wanted to tell us your experiences of Dartford and if you felt we covered every aspect of life there! dartfordsurvivalguide@live.co.uk

Lightning Source UK Ltd.
Milton Keynes UK
UKOW031917250413

209788UK00009B/86/P